Juices & Smoothies

hamlyn

First published in Great Britain in 2003 by Hamlyn,
a division of Octopus Publishing Group Ltd 2–4 Heron Quays, London E14 4JP

Distributed in the United States and Canada by
Sterling Publishing Co., Inc.
387 Park Avenue South, New York, NY 10016-8810

ISBN 0 600 60843 3

A CIP catalogue record for this book is available from the British Library

Printed and bound in China

10 9 8 7 6 5 4 3

All the recipes in this book have been tested using the Oscar Pulverizing Juicer.
If a different juicer is used the quantity of juice may vary.

contents

Introduction

Ask many people what would improve their quality of life, and it is likely that 'more energy' would feature prominently among their answers. We are all aware that food is our main source of energy, and that we should 'eat five' (eat five portions of fruit or vegetables) each day, but many of us don't. Instead, knowingly or otherwise, we undermine the value of food by eating too much of the wrong kinds, and too little of the right kinds, not to mention skipping meals altogether. Home-made juices and smoothies are a simple, delicious and relatively inexpensive way to keep up our intake of the good guys, boosting energy levels, and aiding a general feeling of wellbeing along the way.

What's so great about juices and smoothies?

Fruit and vegetables contain many of the important enzymes, vitamins and minerals that we need to stay healthy, be full of energy and fight off disease. Juicing several types of raw fruits and vegetables daily is an easy – not to mention tasty – way to ensure you receive your full quota of these vital nutrients. Juices contain no fibre or pulp because liquid from the fruit or vegetable is extracted by pressing or squeezing with great force, and discarding any residual pulp. As the juice contains all of the goodness but no hard-to-digest fibre, the nutrients are readily absorbed by the body for almost instant use. Smoothies are thicker and more pulpy as they are a mixture of freshly squeezed juice and some of the crushed fruit, and may also contain other ingredients such as milk or yogurt.

Eat well, look great

All this goodness on the inside will have a positive effect on the outside because feeling fit, healthy and energized really shows. Take antioxidants, for example. They are present in fruits and vegetables and are essential to a younger-looking skin. Also present in many fruits and vegetables is folic acid, which helps to keep hair and nails strong.

Another advantage of drinking juices and smoothies is that they automatically up our intake of water. It is easy to forget to drink enough water and so much of what we drink (tea, coffee, flavoured drinks and alcohol) contains substances that are in themselves dehydrating, but fruit and vegetable juices do not.

Don't forget

Juices and smoothies should be used as part of a sensible eating plan so you must still eat enough from the other food groups (such as grains, dairy foods and pulses). If you are following a special diet, or are under medical supervision, consult your health practitioner before making drastic changes to your health regime.

summer breeze (see page 100)

morning dew (see page 88)

Why make your own juices?

Fresh, home-made juices surpass anything you can buy from supermarkets or even health food stores. Bought juices usually contain additives and preservatives and many don't have much fresh juice in them at all. By making your own, you can choose exactly what ingredients to use, and you have the peace of mind of knowing exactly where they came from. For maximum benefit, drink juices immediately after you've made them as the ingredients deteriorate fast once juiced. If you don't, store leftovers in the refrigerator and consume within 24 hours.

Choosing and preparing ingredients

The quality of a juice is directly related to the freshness of the ingredients. Try to use the best you can get, always choosing those with good colour and optimum ripeness. Organic produce is free from chemical residues and, although it's more expensive, devotees swear by the improved taste and juiciness. Organic ingredients need not be peeled, which is desirable as most vitamins and minerals tend to be lie just below the surface of fruit and vegetable skins (which is also where pesticide residues collect). Prepare ingredients just before using them so that fewer nutrients are lost through oxidization.

Although fresh is usually best, if fruit and vegetables are frozen soon after picking they can be better than fresh produce that is past its best. Summer fruits – strawberries, blueberries and raspberries – are a good example. If you use canned fruit, make sure it is in natural juice or water, not syrup. Dried fruits, in particular apricots, prunes and dates, are a concentrated source of sugars, vitamins and minerals but soak them overnight to make them easier to purée.

To peel or not to peel

Most enzymes, vitamins and minerals lie just below the skins of fruits and vegetables, so include them where possible. If you use organic produce you can leave most skins on, but remember to wash each item thoroughly in warm water first. Generally, it is safer to peel non-organic produce. Always peel avocados, bananas, mangoes, papaya and pineapple. You can leave the skin on unwaxed citrus fruits if some rind is called for in the recipe, but it is more usual to peel them, or squeeze them in a lemon squeezer. Leave the skin on kiwifruit unless the recipe states otherwise.

Remove stones and seeds

Remove large stones such as those in apricots, avocados, mangoes, peaches and plums. Many melon seeds are full of juice, so unless instructed otherwise, include them, with the exception of papaya seeds. Apple and citrus seeds may make the juice bitter, so don't put them in.

Other ingredients

Other ingredients such as milk, yogurt, nuts, seeds and herbal teas make for even more interesting and nutritious drinks. Some recipes contain supplements, which are a concentrated source of essential vitamins and minerals. Spirulina is a form of chlorophyll credited with, among other benefits, halting the signs of ageing. It is good in juices but may spoil their colour. Energizing wheatgrass is also rich in chlorophyll and boosts immunity.

Be creative

Once you have tried some of these recipes, do not be afraid to experiment with some of your own, but follow these simple guidelines:

- Carrots and apples blend well with almost anything.
- Avoid too many strong-tasting vegetables in one juice.
- If using strong- or bitter-tasting vegetables, dilute and sweeten them with carrot and cucumber.

Juicing equipment

You may already own a lemon squeezer and a food processor or blender, but to make the juices in this book you will also need to invest in a specialist juicer which can separate the juice from the pulp of most fruits and vegetables. When choosing, select one that has a big enough opening for larger fruit and vegetables, and one that comes apart for easy cleaning.

Types of juicer

- **Citrus juicer**: commonly known as the humble lemon squeezer, it's ideal for extracting the juice from lemons, limes, oranges and grapefruit. Citrus fruits can be peeled (leaving as much pith on as possible) and juiced as other ingredients if you prefer. Citrus juices are highly acidic and are best diluted, either with other juices or water.
- **Centrifugal juicer**: this is the most widely available and affordable of the specialized juicers on the market: ingredients are fed into a rapidly spinning grater which separates the pulp from the juice by centrifugal force.
- **Masticating juicer**: this type is more expensive but gives a higher yield. The ingredients are pulverized and forced through a fine wire mesh to extract the maximum amount of liquid.
- **Food processor or blender**: this works by puréeing ingredients and is used to make smoothies, as well as to mix crushed ice into some juices. Make sure your blender or food processor is strong enough to crush ice; if it is not, you can use ice-cold water instead.

Cleaning your juicer

It is very important to clean your juicer thoroughly every time you use it to prevent bacterial growth on any pulp residues. Look for a machine that dismantles easily, otherwise cleaning it becomes an annoying task and you may be discouraged from using it. Soak the equipment in warm soapy water and use a new toothbrush or nail brush to get into those awkward corners. A solution of one part white vinegar to two parts water will reduce staining and discoloration.

Classic Smoothies

smooth operator

3 carrots
2 figs
1 orange
2.5 cm (1 inch) cube fresh root ginger, roughly chopped
½ large banana

Place the carrots, figs, orange and ginger in the juicer and whizz together. Put the juice into a blender with the banana and 2 ice cubes and process for 20 seconds. Add more ice cubes and decorate with sliced figs, if liked.

Makes 200 ml (7 fl oz)

apple and blueberry smoothie

2 large apples
125 g (4 oz) blueberries, fresh or frozen

Juice the apple, then whizz in a blender with the blueberries. Serve in a tumbler.

Makes 150 ml (¼ pint)

bugsy banana

1 large carrot
1 small orange
½ large banana
1 dried apricot

Juice the carrot and orange. Whizz in a blender with the banana, apricot and some ice cubes. Decorate with slices of banana, if liked.

Makes 200 ml (7 fl oz)

super shakey

½ pineapple, about 225 g (7½ oz)
½ parsnip
1 carrot
75 ml (3 fl oz) soya milk

Juice the pineapple, parsnip and carrot. Whizz in a blender with the soya milk and a couple of ice cubes. Decorate with pineapple wedges, if liked.

Makes 200 ml (7 fl oz)

smooth operator

apple and blueberry smoothie

rocket fuel

1 ripe mango
300 ml (½ pint) pineapple juice
rind and juice of ½ lime

Roughly chop the mango flesh and freeze for at least 2 hours or overnight. Place the frozen mango in a blender with the pineapple juice and lime rind and juice and process until thick. Decorate with lime wedges, if liked.

Makes 400 ml (14 fl oz)

high flyer

1 ripe mango
200 ml (7 fl oz) cranberry juice
150 g (5 oz) peach yogurt

Roughly chop the mango flesh and place in a blender with the cranberry juice and yogurt. Process until smooth and pour into a glass. Add a couple of ice cubes and decorate with fresh cranberries, if liked.

Makes 400 ml (14 fl oz)

banana and peanut butter smoothie

1 ripe banana
300 ml (½ pint) semi-skimmed milk
1 tablespoon smooth peanut butter or 2 teaspoons tahini paste

Peel and slice the banana and freeze for at least 2 hours or overnight. Put the banana, milk and peanut butter or tahini paste in a blender and process until smooth.

Makes 400 ml (14 fl oz)

maybe baby

1 pear
½ avocado

Juice the pear, and then blend it with the avocado. Pour into a glass, and add a couple of ice cubes.

Makes 150 ml (¼ pint)

rocket fuel

high flyer

round the clock

1 small ripe avocado
1 small ripe banana
250 ml (8 fl oz) skimmed milk

Roughly chop the avocado flesh and slice the banana. Place with the milk in a blender and process to make a high-energy smoothie. Pour into a glass, and add a couple of ice cubes.

Makes 400 ml (14 fl oz)

prune, apple and cinnamon smoothie

65 g (2½ oz) ready-to-eat prunes
pinch of ground cinnamon
350 ml (12 fl oz) apple juice
3 tablespoons Greek yogurt

Roughly chop the prunes and place with the cinnamon in a large bowl. Pour over the apple juice, cover and allow to stand overnight. Place the prune and apple juice mixture with the yogurt in a blender and process until smooth. Pour into a glass, add ice cubes and sprinkle with cinnamon, if liked.

Makes 400 ml (14 fl oz)

jumping jack

2 very ripe bananas
450 ml (¾ pint) soya milk
40 g (1½ oz) ground almonds
pinch of ground cinnamon
a little honey (optional)

Slice the bananas and freeze for at least 2 hours or overnight. Place the frozen bananas, soya milk, ground almonds and cinnamon in a blender, add the honey, if using, and process until thick and frothy. Pour into glasses, add a couple of ice cubes and decorate with ground cinnamon, if liked.

Makes 600 ml (1 pint)

summer berry smoothie

150 g (5 oz) frozen mixed summer berries
300 ml (½ pint) vanilla-flavoured soya milk
1 teaspoon clear honey (optional)

Place the berries, soya milk and honey, if using, in a blender and process until thick. Serve immediately, decorated with berries if liked.

Makes 400 ml (14 fl oz)

round the clock

jumping jack

summer berry smoothie

peach and orange smoothie

400 g (13 oz) can peaches in natural juice, drained
150 g (5 oz) peach or apricot yogurt
200 ml (7 fl oz) orange juice
a little honey (optional)

Place the peaches in a blender with the yogurt, orange juice and honey, if using, and process until smooth. Add a couple of ice cubes, and decorate with slices of peach, if liked.

Makes 500 ml (17 fl oz)

rhubarb and custard smoothie

150 g (5 oz) can rhubarb
150 g (5 oz) carton ready-made custard
100 ml (3½ fl oz) semi-skimmed milk, ice-cold
1 teaspoon icing sugar (optional)

Drain the rhubarb then put it into a blender with the custard, milk and icing sugar, if using, and process until smooth. Pour into a glass, and add a couple of ice cubes, if liked.

Makes 400 ml (14 fl oz)

all nighter

1 small ripe banana
75 g (3 oz) strawberries, hulled
250 ml (8 fl oz) orange juice

Slice the banana and roughly chop the strawberries. Freeze the fruit for at least 2 hours or overnight. Place the frozen fruit and the orange juice in a blender and process until thick. Decorate with strawberries, if liked.

Makes 400 ml (14 fl oz)

big boost

65 g (2½ oz) dried apricots
350 ml (12 fl oz) pineapple juice

Roughly chop the apricots into small pieces and put them in a large bowl. Pour the pineapple juice over them, cover the bowl and allow to stand overnight. Tip the contents into a blender and process until smooth. Serve in a glass with a couple of ice cubes, if liked.

Makes 350 ml (12 fl oz)

peach and orange smoothie

all nighter

big boost

blackberry and grape smoothie

125 g (4 oz) frozen blackberries
300 ml (½ pint) purple grape juice
3 tablespoons quark or fromage frais
1 teaspoon clear honey (optional)

Put the blackberries, grape juice and quark or fromage frais in a food processor or blender, add the honey, if using, and process until thick. Decorate with blackberries, if liked.

Makes 350 ml (12 fl oz)

apple pie

100 ml (3½ fl oz) apple juice
100 g (3½ oz) canned custard
ground cinnamon, to taste

Blend the ice-cold apple juice and custard until smooth then serve sprinkled with cinnamon.

Makes 200 ml (7 fl oz)

banana and mango smoothie

1 ripe banana
1 ripe mango
200 ml (7 fl oz) orange juice
200 ml (7 fl oz) semi-skimmed milk
3 tablespoons fromage frais

Slice the banana and roughly chop the mango flesh. Put with the orange juice, milk and fromage frais into a blender and process until smooth. Pour into a glass, and add a couple of ice cubes to chill.

Makes 500 ml (17 fl oz)

fruit smoothie

1 papaya
1 orange
1 banana
300 ml (½ pint) apple juice

Halve and deseed the papaya. Scoop out the flesh, cut the orange into segments and whizz together with the chopped banana in a blender. Add the mixture to the apple juice and stir well. Serve with ice, if liked.

Makes 400 ml (14 fl oz)

blackberry and grape smoothie

apple pie

kiwifruit, melon and passion fruit smoothie

¼ watermelon, about 300 g (10 oz) flesh
2 kiwifruit
200 ml (7 fl oz) passion fruit juice

Remove and discard the seeds from the watermelon and dice the flesh. Freeze for at least 2 hours or overnight. Peel and roughly chop the kiwifruit and place them in a blender with the watermelon and the passion fruit juice and process until thick. Decorate with passion fruit seeds, if liked.

Makes 400 ml (14 fl oz)

quick hit

125 g (4 oz) strawberries, hulled
1 small ripe mango
300 ml (½ pint) orange juice

Roughly chop the strawberries and the mango flesh and freeze for at least 2 hours or overnight. Place them in a blender with the orange juice and process until thick. Decorate with slices of mango, if liked.

Makes 400 ml (14 fl oz)

strawberry and pineapple smoothie

150 g (5 oz) strawberries, hulled
150 ml (¼ pint) pineapple juice
150 g (5 oz) strawberry yogurt

Roughly chop the strawberries, and freeze for at least 2 hours or overnight. Place the frozen strawberries, pineapple juice and yogurt in a blender and process until smooth. Pour into a glass, add a couple of ice cubes, and decorate with strawberries, if liked.

Makes 400 ml (14 fl oz)

bionic tonic

1 large banana
1 large ripe mango
150 g (5 oz) natural bio yogurt
300 ml (½ pint) pineapple juice

Slice the banana and roughly chop the mango flesh. Freeze for at least 2 hours or overnight. Place the frozen banana and mango in a blender with the yogurt and pineapple juice. Process until smooth, serve in a glass and decorate with pineapple chunks, if liked.

Makes 600 ml (1 pint)

kiwifruit, melon and passion fruit smoothie

quick hit

bionic tonic

sleeping beauty

200 ml (7 fl oz) soya milk
2 kiwifruit
100 g (3½ oz) fresh or frozen strawberries, hulled
25 g (1 oz) flaked almonds

Put all the ingredients in a food processor or blender. If using fresh rather than frozen strawberries add a few ice cubes, then process until smooth. Pour into a glass and decorate with flaked almonds, if liked.

Makes 300 ml (½ pint)

nutty professor

250 ml (8 fl oz) semi-skimmed milk
½ large banana
½ large mango
1 tablespoon peanut butter

Blend together all the ingredients with a couple of ice cubes for a silky, satisfying smoothie. To serve decorate with slices of mango.

Makes 300 ml (½ pint)

hippy shake

½ pineapple, about 225 g (7½ oz)
1 lemon
½ large avocado

Roughly chop the pineapple flesh and juice with the peeled lemon. Place the juice into a blender with the avocado and process until smooth. Serve with a slice of lemon, if liked.

Makes 200 ml (7 fl oz)

dried fruit salad smoothie

125 g (4 oz) dried fruit salad
400 ml (14 fl oz) apple juice, more if necessary
200 ml (7 fl oz) Greek yogurt

Roughly chop the fruit and place it in a large bowl. Pour over the apple juice, cover and allow to stand overnight. Put the dried fruit salad and apple juice in a food processor or blender, add the yogurt and process until smooth, adding a little more apple juice if necessary. Pour into a glass and add a couple of ice cubes to chill.

Makes 450 ml (¾ pint)

hippy shake

nutty professor

raspberry ripple

100 g (3½ oz) fresh raspberries
100 g (3½ oz) natural yogurt
100 ml (3½ fl oz) soya milk

Whizz the raspberries, natural yogurt and soya milk together in a blender until smooth. Swirl in a little yogurt to decorate.

Makes 300 ml (½ pint)

energy store

200 ml (7 fl oz) canned peaches in grape juice
100 ml (3½ fl oz) soya milk
15 g (½ oz) sunflower seeds

Put the peaches and their juice in a blender with the soya milk and sunflower seeds and process for about 20 seconds until smooth. Add a few ice cubes and blend again for about 10 seconds. Decorate with peach slices to serve.

Makes 300 ml (½ pint)

cranberry, banana and sesame smoothie

40 g (1½ oz) dried cranberries
½ lemon, juice only
1 large banana
1 tablespoon sesame seeds
2 tablespoons Greek yogurt
200 ml (7 fl oz) whole or semi-skimmed milk

Process the cranberries and lemon juice in a blender until the berries are finely chopped. Add the banana and sesame seeds then purée, scraping the mixture down from the sides of the bowl if necessary. Add the yogurt and milk, processing until smooth and frothy. Decorate with dried cranberries, if liked.

Makes 300 ml (½ pint)

apricot smoothie

200 g (7 oz) canned of apricots in natural juice, drained
150 g (5 oz) apricot yogurt
150 ml (¼ pint) ice-cold semi-skimmed milk

Place the apricots, yogurt and milk in a food processor or blender and process until smooth. Add a couple of ice cubes, pour into a glass and decorate with slices of apricot, if liked.

Makes 400 ml (14 fl oz)

raspberry ripple

energy store

cranberry, banana and sesame smoothie

Tropical Teasers

hi tension *(see page 36)*

hula kula

½ pineapple, about 215 g (7 oz)
100 ml (3½ fl oz) coconut milk
100 ml (3½ fl oz) soya milk

Place all the ingredients in a blender with some ice cubes and blend until the mixture is smooth. Decorate with pineapple leaves, if liked.

Makes 300 ml (½ pint)

sour grapes

100 g (3½ oz) green or black grapes
100 ml (3½ fl oz) cranberry juice
100 g (3½ oz) pitted cherries

Juice the grapes then blend with the other ingredients. Serve over ice and decorate with fresh cherries, if liked.

Makes 250 ml (8 fl oz)

bollywood blaster

¼ pineapple, about 100 g (3½ oz)
½ small grapefruit
½ large banana

Juice the pineapple and grapefruit. Put the juice into a blender with the banana and whizz.

Makes 250 ml (8 fl oz)

lounge lizard

2½ kiwifruits
125 g (4 oz) cucumber
1 tablespoon pomegranate seeds (if available)

Juice the kiwifruit and cucumber for a high vitamin C drink. Serve with a slice of lime, to decorate. If you wish, stir in a tablespoon of pomegranate seeds.

Makes 150 ml (¼ pint)

lounge lizard

sour grapes

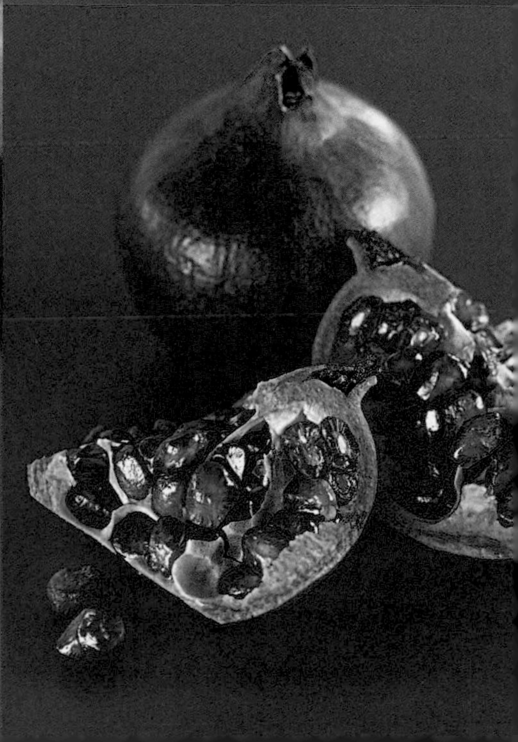

silver cloud

½ lemon
100 ml (3½ fl oz) soya milk
50 g (2 oz) ground almonds
100 g (3½ oz) canned lychees (drained weight)

Juice the lemon and put it into a blender with the other ingredients and an ice cube. Blend until smooth and frothy. Serve decorated with lemon peel, if liked.

Makes 200 ml (7 fl oz)

mandarin oriental

1 large apple
75 g (3 oz) canned mandarin segments (drained weight)
75 g (3 oz) canned lychees (drained weight)

Juice the apple then blender with the mandarins and lychees. Add an ice cube and blend until smooth. Serve with ice cubes and mandarin segments, if liked.

Makes 250 ml (8 fl oz)

melonberry

⅛ watermelon, about 150 g (5 oz) flesh
150 g (5 oz) raspberries

Juice both fruits and serve over ice. Alternatively, whizz in a blender with ice to make a fruity slush. Serve decorated with mint, if liked.

Makes 200 ml (7 fl oz)

drama queen

¼ watermelon, about 300 g (10 oz) flesh
1 pomegranate
100 g (3½ oz) raspberries

Scoop out the flesh of the melon and the pomegranate seeds. Juice with the raspberries and serve over ice. Decorate with pomegranate seeds, if liked.

Makes 200 ml (7 fl oz)

mandarin oriental

drama queen

mango lassi

½ large mango
100 ml (3½ fl oz) natural yogurt
100 ml (3½ fl oz) water

Blend the mango flesh with the other ingredients until smooth then serve decorated with mint.

Makes 350 ml (12 fl oz)

atomic tonic

1 orange
½ lemon
½ large mango
100 g (3½ oz) canned mandarins (drained weight)

Juice the orange and lemon and then blend with the mango flesh and mandarins. Serve poured over ice and decorated with a basil leaf, if liked.

Makes 300 ml (½ pint)

free spirit

200 g (7 oz) lettuce
1 large pear
2 kiwifruit

Juice all the ingredients and serve over ice decorated with a slice of lemon, if liked.

Makes 300 ml (½ pint)

choc berry

50 g (2 oz) chocolate and hazelnut spread
50 g (2 oz) frozen strawberries
100 g (3½ oz) canned custard
100 ml (3½ fl oz) soya milk

Whizz all the ingredients together in a blender until smooth and serve immediately. Decorate with a strawberry, to serve.

Makes 250 ml (8 fl oz)

mountain dreamer

½ large pink grapefruit
100 g (3½ oz) canned lychees (drained weight)

Juice the grapefruit and place in a blender with the lychees. Blend until smooth. Pour into a glass and decorate with a slice of grapefruit, if liked.

Makes 200 ml (7 fl oz)

choc berry

mango lassi

mountain dreamer

fruit frappe

1 peach
1 pomegranate

Discard the peach stone and the skin of the pomegranate. Juice both ingredients and then blend with 2 or 3 ice cubes.

Makes 200 ml (7 fl oz)

punchball

2 celery sticks
100 g (3½ oz) green grapes
½ small avocado

Juice the celery and grapes. Put the juice into a blender with the avocado and serve with a couple of ice cubes and a celery leaf, if liked.

Makes 200 ml (7 fl oz)

key lime pie

1 kiwifruit
½ lime
100 ml (3½ fl oz) soya milk

Juice the kiwifruit and the lime. Transfer to a blender and whizz with an ice cube and the soya milk.

Makes 200 ml (7 fl oz)

berry springer

100 g (3½ oz) frozen mixed berries
100 g (3½ oz) canned lychees (drained weight)
100 g (3½ oz) coconut milk
100 ml (3½ fl oz) soya milk

Put all the ingredients in a blender with a couple of ice cubes and blend until smooth.

Makes 200 ml (7 fl oz)

blockbuster

25 g (1 oz) each of papaya, pineapple, carrot, sweet potato, apple, melon, grapefruit and celery.

Juice all the ingredients together and serve in a tall glass over ice. Decorate with slices of apple.

Makes 250 ml (8 fl oz)

berry springer

blockbuster

punchball

moody blues

375 g (12 oz) blackberries
1 small pineapple, about 375 g (12 oz)

Juice the blackberries first, then the pineapple. Blend the juices together with a couple of ice cubes and serve in a tall glass, decorated with a pineapple sliver, if liked.

Makes 200 ml (7 fl oz)

frisky sour

½ papaya
½ grapefruit
150 g (5 oz) raspberries
½ lime

Juice the flesh of the papaya with the grapefruit (pith left on) and the raspberries. Squeeze in the lime juice and mix together. Serve with a few ice cubes and, if liked, decorate with lime slices.

Makes 200 ml (7 fl oz)

hi tension

¼ pineapple, about 150 g (5 oz)
3 celery sticks
½ lemon

Juice all the ingredients then serve over ice in a tall glass. Decorate with sprigs of mint, if liked.

Makes 200 ml (7 fl oz)

love potion no. 9

½ lime
1 small apple
1 passion fruit
¼ papaya

Juice the lime, apple and passion fruit pulp. Put the juice into a food processor or blender with the papaya flesh and blend until smooth.

Makes 200 ml (7 fl oz)

hi tension

moody blues

frisky sour

banana calmer

1 small banana
2 large oranges, juice only
25 g (1 oz) sunflower seeds

Put the banana, orange juice and sunflower seeds into a blender with a few ice cubes and process until smooth. Serve in a large tumbler and decorate with some strawberry halves, if liked.

Makes 300 ml (½ pint)

acher shaker

100 g (3½ oz) strawberries
½ pineapple, about 250 g (8 oz)
1 banana

Juice the strawberries and pineapple. Pour the juice into a blender, add the banana and a couple of ice cubes and process. Serve decorated with pineapple slices, if liked.

Makes 300 ml (½ pint)

cool juice

100 g (3½ oz) strawberries
¼ watermelon, about 300 g (10 oz) flesh
75 g (3 oz) cucumber

Juice the strawberries, melon flesh and cucumber. Serve over ice in a tall glass, decorated with cucumber slices, if liked.

Makes 200 ml (7 fl oz)

ocher shaker

banana calmer

cool juice

time out

¼ cantaloupe melon
100 g (3½ oz) fresh or frozen blackberries
2 kiwifruit

Juice the melon flesh, blackberries and kiwifruit, then put the juices in a blender and process with a couple of ice cubes. Pour into a glass and serve decorated with a few blackberries, if liked.

Makes 250 ml (8 fl oz)

cucumber and mint lassi

200 g (7 oz) cucumber
250 g (8 oz) natural bio yogurt
handful of chopped mint
¼ teaspoon salt (optional)

Remove and discard the cucumber seeds. Place the flesh in a blender with the yogurt, mint and salt, if using, and process until smooth. Pour into a glass, add a couple of ice cubes and decorate with mint, if liked.

Makes 300 ml (½ pint)

wacky whizzard

½ large mango
2 small apples
125 g (4 oz) cucumber

Juice the ingredients then blend with a couple of ice cubes to make a fruity slush.

Makes 200 ml (7 fl oz)

mango, orange and soya milkshake

1 small mango
1 orange, juice only
150 ml (¼ pint) soya milk
1–2 teaspoons honey

Scoop the mango flesh into a blender with the orange juice, soya milk and 1 teaspoon of honey. Process until smooth, scraping the sides if necessary. Taste for sweetness, and add more honey, if liked.

Makes 300 ml (½ pint)

neuro zen

200 g (7 oz) white grapes
200 g (7 oz) lettuce
2.5 cm (1 inch) cube fresh root ginger, roughly chopped

Juice all the ingredients. Serve over ice, or pour into a blender and process with ice cubes for a zingy icy slush. Decorate with white or red grapes, if liked.

Makes 200 ml (7 fl oz)

time out

wacky wizzard

neuro zen

Veggie Juices

green light

100 g (3½ oz) broccoli
1 small apple
100 g (3½ oz) cucumber

Juice the broccoli with the apple and cucumber and serve in a tall glass. Decorate with cucumber slivers, if liked.

Makes 200 ml (7 fl oz)

cool down

2 small carrots
2 beetroot, about 100 g (3½ oz)
½ yam or 1 small sweet potato
1 small bulb fennel

Juice all the ingredients. Mix the energy-boosting juices together and serve in a glass with ice cubes. Decorate with fennel fronds, if liked.

Makes 200 ml (7 fl oz)

six pack

125 g (4 oz) asparagus spears
10 dandelion leaves
¼ Galia or honeydew melon
175 g (6 oz) cucumber
1 large pear

Trim the woody bits off the asparagus spears. Roll the dandelion leaves into a ball and juice them (if you have picked wild leaves, wash them first) with the asparagus. Juice the melon flesh, cucumber and pear. Whizz all the juices in a blender and serve in a tall glass with ice cubes.

Makes 200 ml (7 fl oz)

root 66

2 small carrots
1 parsnip
3 celery sticks
1 small sweet potato
a handful of parsley
1 garlic clove

Juice all the ingredients together then whizz in a blender with 2 ice cubes. Serve in a short glass decorated with a wedge of lemon and a parsley sprig, if liked.

Makes 200 ml (7 fl oz)

six pack

cool down

root 66

hot stuff

2 medium tomatoes, about 350 g (12 oz)
2 celery sticks
2.5 cm (1 inch) cube fresh root ginger, roughly chopped
1 garlic clove
2.5 cm (1 inch) cube fresh horseradish
2 small carrots

Juice all the ingredients, then blend with 2 ice cubes and serve in a tumbler. Decorate with celery slivers, if liked.

Makes 150 ml (¼ pint)

earth mother

1 carrot
125 g (4 oz) lettuce
1 small parsnip
¼ cantaloupe melon

Juice the carrot, lettuce and parsnip with the flesh of the melon. Mix thoroughly and serve in a tall glass with ice and wedges of melon, if liked.

Makes 250 ml (8 fl oz)

loosen up 1

4 cm (1½ inch) cube fresh horseradish
½ lemon, juice only

Pulverize the horseradish by juicing a small amount and mixing the juice and the pulp to make about 1½ teaspoons of purée. Put it into a shot glass and stir in the lemon juice.

Makes 50 ml (2 fl oz)

loosen up 2

2 small carrots
100 g (3½ oz) radishes, with tops and leaves
2.5 cm (1 inch) cube fresh root ginger, roughly chopped (optional)

Juice the carrots, radishes and ginger, if using. Add some ice cubes. Drink one hour after Loosen Up 1.

Makes 200 ml (7 fl oz)

These two juices are great if you have a cold and should be taken in tandum.

hot stuff

earth mother

loosen up 2

loosen up 1

heart beet

2 large beetroot, about 125 g (4 oz)
125 g (4 oz) watercress
1 small red onion
3 small carrots
1 garlic clove

Juice all the ingredients and serve mixed together in a tall glass. Garnish with beet leaves and watercress, if liked.

Makes 200 ml (7 fl oz)

head banger

175 g (6 oz) lettuce
1 small bulb fennel
½ lemon

Juice the lettuce, fennel and lemon. Mix well and serve poured over ice. Decorate with lemon rind slivers and lettuce leaves, if liked.

Makes 150 ml (¼ pint)

famous 5

100 g (3½ oz) Brussels sprouts
1 carrot
100 g (3½ oz) Jerusalem artichokes
100 g (3½ oz) green beans
100 g (3½ oz) lettuce
½ lemon

Juice all the vegetables together with the lemon. Serve garnished with slivers of green bean and carrot, if liked.

Makes 200 ml (7 fl oz)

head banger

heart beet

famous 5

iron maiden

250 g (8 oz) spinach
25 g (1 oz) parsley
3 small carrots
1 teaspoon spirulina

Juice the spinach, parsley and carrots and stir in the spirulina. Serve in a tumbler, garnished with carrot slivers if liked.

Makes 200 ml (7 fl oz)

sleep tight

¼ pineapple, about 125 g (4 oz)
125 g (4 oz) grapes
50 g (2 oz) lettuce
1 stick celery

Juice all the ingredients and serve in a tall glass over ice. Decorate with lettuce leaves, if liked.

Makes 200 ml (7 fl oz)

well healed

3 small carrots
250 g (8 oz) green cabbage

Juice the vegetables and serve in a tall glass, over ice. Garnish with a few shreds of cabbage.

Makes 200 ml (7 fl oz)

sticks and stones

125 g (4 oz) turnips, including the tops
1 carrot
125 g (4 oz) broccoli
handful of dandelion leaves
2 small apples

Juice all the ingredients then whizz in a blender with a couple of ice cubes. Serve in a tall glass decorated with dandelion leaves, if liked.

Makes 200 ml (7 fl oz)

iron maiden

hot potato

1 small potato, cooked
100 g (3½ oz) radish
1 small carrot
100 g (3½ oz) cucumber

Juice the ingredients together and then whizz in a blender with 2 ice cubes. Serve in a tall glass garnished with radish slices, if liked.

Makes 200 ml (7 fl oz)

twister

½ pink grapefruit
1 large carrot
125 g (4 oz) spinach

Peel the grapefruit, keeping as much of the pith as possible. Juice all the ingredients and serve in a tumbler, decorated with grapefruit slices, if liked.

Makes 200 ml (7 fl oz)

hard as nails

1 small parsnip
1 green pepper, seeded
100 g (3½ oz) watercress
175 g (6 oz) cucumber

Juice the ingredients together and serve over ice with a sprinkling of mint, if liked.

Makes 200 ml (7 fl oz)

herbi-four

1 red pepper, seeded
1 tomato, about 175 g (6 oz)
100 g (3½ oz) white cabbage
1 tablespoon chopped parsley

Juice the pepper, tomato and cabbage. Pour into a tall glass, stir in the parsley and serve with ice cubes and a lime wedge, if liked.

Makes 200 ml (7 fl oz)

twister

herbi-four

hot potato

hard as nails

vision impeccable

2 small carrots
125 g (4 oz) endive
2 celery sticks

Juice the carrot, endive and celery. Whizz in a food processor or blender with a couple of ice cubes and serve over ice garnished with lemon slices and some chopped parsley, if liked.

Makes 200 ml (7 fl oz)

what's up broc?

250 g (8 oz) broccoli
2 small carrots
1 small beetroot, about 50 g (2 oz)

Juice all the ingredients together and then serve in a tall glass. Add crushed ice and garnish with a coriander sprig, if liked.

Makes 200 ml (7 fl oz)

chilli queen

2 carrots
½ small deseeded chilli or a sprinkling of chilli powder
½ pineapple, about 225 g (7½ oz)
½ lime, juice only
1 tablespoon chopped coriander leaves

Juice the carrots, chilli and pineapple. Pour into a tall glass over ice cubes. Squeeze in the lime juice and stir in the chopped coriander leaves to serve.

Makes 200 ml (7 fl oz)

hangover express

150 g (5 oz) broccoli
2 apples
150 g (5 oz) spinach

Juice the broccoli, apples and spinach, alternating the spinach leaves with the broccoli and apple to prevent the machine from clogging up with the leaves. Blend the juice with a couple of ice cubes, and serve with ice and a slice of lemon, if liked.

Makes 200 ml (7 fl oz)

vision impeccable

chilli queen

hangover express

what's up doc?

tranquillizer

175 g (6 oz) Romaine lettuce
2 apples

Juice the lettuce and apples. Place ice cubes in a tall glass and pour the juice over them. Serve immediately, decorated with apple slices, if liked.

Makes 200 ml (7 fl oz)

stress buster

150 g (5 oz) spinach
150 g (5 oz) broccoli
2 tomatoes

Juice the spinach, broccoli and tomatoes then mix together. Serve in a tumbler over ice, decorated with sliced tomatoes, if liked.

Makes 200 ml (7 fl oz)

squeaky green

2 carrots
2 celery sticks
100 g (3½ oz) spinach
100 g (3½ oz) lettuce
25 g (1 oz) parsley

Juice the ingredients and whizz in a blender with a couple of ice cubes. Garnish with parsley sprigs, if liked.

Makes 200 ml (7 fl oz)

veg out

100 g (3½ oz) cauliflower
2 small carrots
1 large tomato

Juice the cauliflower, carrots and tomato. Stir to mix then serve poured over ice and garnished with carrot tops, if liked.

Makes 200 ml (7 fl oz)

squeaky green

veg out

upbeet

100 g (3½ oz) celeriac, peeled
1 beetroot, about 50 g (2 oz)
1 carrot
50 g (2 oz) radicchio
1 apple

Juice all the ingredients, then process the juice in a blender with a couple of ice cubes. Garnish with slivers of radicchio, if liked.

Makes 200 ml (7 fl oz)

gargle blaster

100 g (3½ oz) celeriac
100 g (3½ oz) Jerusalem artichokes
2 celery sticks
small bunch of mint

Juice the vegetables and the mint, alternating the mint leaves with the other ingredients to prevent the juicer getting clogged up. Process the juice in a blender with ice cubes and serve garnished with celery sticks, if liked.

Makes 200 ml (7 fl oz)

spring clean

2 small pears
125 g (4 oz) cabbage
1 celery stick
25 g (1 oz) watercress

Juice all the ingredients together. Serve over ice garnished with celery sticks, if liked.

Makes 200 ml (7 fl oz)

go with the flow

3 celery sticks
25 g (1 oz) rocket
25 g (1 oz) watercress
1 apple
½ small avocado

Juice the celery, rocket, watercress and apple. Put the juice in a blender with the avocado and a couple of ice cubes and process until smooth. Garnish with a slice of lime, if liked.

Makes 200 ml (7 fl oz)

spring clean

upbeet

go with the flow

Citrus Juices

the rehydrator (see page [illegible])

navel cadet

1 lime
2 small oranges
½ large mango

Juice the lime and oranges and whizz in a food processor or blender together with the mango flesh and an ice cube. Decorate with lime slices, if liked.

Makes 250 ml (8 fl oz)

bitter sweet

½ large grapefruit
1 small parsnip
1 small sweet potato

Juice all the ingredients and blend the juice with an ice cube. Serve in over ice and, if liked, decorate with a sliver of parsnip.

Makes 200 ml (7 fl oz)

karma fruitra

½ grapefruit
2 fresh figs
½ small orange
½ lemon

Juice all the fruit then blend with an ice cube to chill. Decorate with slices of fig, if liked.

Makes 200 ml (7 fl oz)

chill pill

1 small fennel bulb
1 lemon
100 ml (3½ fl oz) chilled chamomile tea

Juice the fennel and lemon, then mix with the chamomile tea. Serve over ice with some lemon slices, if liked.

Makes 200 ml (7 fl oz)

karma fruitra

naval cadet

ginger zinger

1 carrot
½ Galia or honeydew melon
1 lime
2.5 cm (1 inch) cube fresh root ginger, roughly chopped

Juice the carrot, melon flesh, lime and ginger. Serve in a glass over ice. Decorate with lime wedges and seeds from a cardamom pod, if liked.

Makes 200 ml (7 fl oz)

sergeant pepper

½ red pepper, deseeded
½ yellow pepper, deseeded
½ orange pepper, deseeded
1 orange
1 tablespoon mint leaves

Juice the peppers and orange and serve in a tumbler with ice cubes. Stir in the mint and decorate with more mint leaves, if liked.

Makes 200 ml (7 fl oz)

carrot and pink grapefruit

1 pink grapefruit
2 carrots
2 apples
400 ml (14 fl oz) water

Juice the carrots, apples and grapefruit then add the water. Pour the juice into a glass and add a couple of ice cubes. Decorate with apple slices, if liked.

Makes 750 ml (1¼ pints)

all systems go

¼ watermelon, about 300 g (10 oz) flesh
2 oranges

Juice the fruit, pour it into a glass and add a couple of ice cubes to chill. Decorate with slices of orange, if liked.

Makes 300 ml (½ pint)

ginger zinger

all systems go

sergeant pepper

pear and pineapple

2 pears
½ lime
½ pineapple, about 200 g (7 oz)

Juice all the fruit. Then, pour into a glass. Add some ice cubes and decorate with wedges of pineapple, if liked.

Makes 300 ml (½ pint)

strawberry, redcurrant and orange

100 g (3½ oz) strawberries, hulled
75 g (3 oz) redcurrants, hulled
½ orange
125 ml (4 fl oz) water
½ teaspoon clear honey (optional)

Juice the fruit, then add the water. Pour into a glass, stir in the honey, if using, and add some ice cubes to create a refreshing fatigue-defying drink. Decorate with redcurrants, if liked.

Makes 250 ml (8 fl oz)

live wire

2 oranges
1 red apple
1 pear
1 teaspoon clear honey (optional)

Juice the fruit and pour it into a glass. Stir in the honey, if using, and add a couple of ice cubes. Decorate with orange slices, if liked.

Makes 350 ml (12 fl oz)

orange and raspberry

2 large oranges
175 g (6 oz) raspberries
250 ml (8 fl oz) water

Juice the fruit then add the water to dilute. Pour into 2 glasses and add a couple of ice cubes to each.

Makes 500 ml (17 fl oz)

live wire

strawberry, redcurrant and orange

orange and apricot

6 apricots, about 300 g (10 oz)
1 large orange
300 ml (½ pint) water

Juice the fruit then add the water. Pour into a glass and add ice cubes to chill, if liked.

Makes 600 ml (1 pint)

sweet chariot

¼ pineapple, about 100 g (3½ oz)
100 g (3½ oz) grapes
1 small orange
1 small apple
½ large mango
½ large banana

Juice the pineapple, grapes, orange and apple. Whizz in a blender with the mango, banana and a couple of ice cubes for a super sweet smoothie. Serve decorated with orange wedges and strips of mint, if liked.

Makes 400 ml (14 fl oz)

orange, cranberry and mango

125 g (4 oz) cranberries
1 mango
1 orange
100 ml (3½ fl oz) water
1 teaspoon clear honey

Juice the fruit, pour into a glass and stir in the water and honey. Add a couple of ice cubes to chill and decorate with cranberries, if liked.

Makes 400 ml (14 fl oz)

citron xpresse

1 lemon
100 g (3½ oz) green grapes

Juice both ingredients then make up to 200 ml (7 fl oz) with cold water. Serve over ice. If you like, add hot water instead to make a hot toddy.

Makes 200 ml (7 fl oz)

karma kooler

2 grapefruit
750 g (1½ lb) cucumber
1 lemon
sparkling mineral water

Juice the grapefruit, cucumber and lemon. Pour into a jug over ice, and top up with sparkling mineral water to make up to 400 ml (14 fl oz). Decorate with mint and slices of cucumber and lemon, if liked.

Makes 400 ml (14 fl oz)

citron xpresse

karma kooler

sweet chariot

pulpitation

1 large orange
½ grapefruit
1 lime

Juice the fruit (and a little of the pith), then serve poured over ice. If you want a longer drink, dilute with an equal amount of sparkling mineral water. Decorate with curls of lime rind, if liked.

Makes 200 ml (7 fl oz)

mind bath

100 g (3½ oz) Romaine lettuce
½ lemon
100 ml (3½ fl oz) chilled chamomile tea

Juice the lettuce and lemon then mix with the chilled chamomile tea. Serve in a tall glass over ice with slices of lemon, if liked.

Makes 200 ml (7 fl oz)

the rehydrator

1 orange
50 g (2 oz) cucumber
100 ml (3½ fl oz) cranberry juice

Juice the orange (with as much of its pith as possible) and cucumber. Mix this juice with the cranberry juice. Serve in a tall glass over ice, decorated with slices of cucumber, if liked.

Makes 200 ml (7 fl oz)

pulpitation

the rehydrator

mind bath

calm seas

2 oranges
1 kiwifruit
200 g (7 oz) strawberries

Juice the oranges (with as much of their pith as possible) with the kiwifruit (skin left on) and the strawberries. Decorate with strawberry slices.

Makes 200 ml (7 fl oz)

c double

2 large oranges
2 kiwifruit

Juice the oranges (with as much of their pith as possible) with the kiwifruit (skins left on). Serve over ice with some kiwifruit slices, if liked.

Makes 200 ml (7 fl oz)

vitamin vitality

1 carrot
2 oranges

Juice the carrot with the oranges and serve decorated with a slice of orange.

Makes 200 ml (7 fl oz)

mother nature

½ grapefruit
2 celery sticks
1 small fennel bulb

Juice the grapefruit, celery and fennel and serve in a tall glass over ice with a slice of pink grapefruit, if liked.

Makes 200 ml (7 fl oz)

butterfly kiss

¼ Galia or honeydew melon
1 lemon
2.5 cm (1 inch) cube fresh root ginger, roughly chopped

Juice the melon flesh, the lemon and the ginger, and serve over ice.

Makes 200 ml (7 fl oz)

double

vitamin vitality

mother nature

Breakfast in a Glass

morning dew (see page 88)

plum punch

1 peach
2 plums
1 kiwifruit

Juice all the ingredients and serve over ice cubes. Decorate with plum slices, if liked.

Makes 200 ml (7 fl oz)

sour power

1 pomegranate
1 carrot
100 g (3½ oz) grapes

Scoop out the pomegranate pulp and seeds then juice with the carrot and grapes. Serve with crushed ice and decorate with pomegranate seeds, if liked.

Makes 200 ml (7 fl oz)

green dream

2 large apples
1 celery stick
½ kiwifruit
½ lemon
1 small avocado

Juice the apple, celery, kiwifruit and lemon. Transfer to a blender and whizz with the avocado for 20 seconds to make a refreshing smoothie. Decorate with kiwi slices, if liked.

Makes 200 ml (7 fl oz)

sour power

plum punch

kiwi quencher

1 kiwifruit
100 g (3½ oz) grapes
2 celery sticks
½ lemon

Juice all the ingredients together and serve poured over ice. If liked, decorate with celery slices.

Makes 150 ml (¼ pint)

papaya flyer

½ large pear
1 carrot
¼ papaya

Juice the pear and carrot and put in a blender with the papaya and an ice cube and blend until smooth. Decorate with thin slices of pear, if liked.

Makes 200 ml (7 fl oz)

mellow yellow

1 small apple
2 celery sticks
100 g (3½ oz) alfalfa sprouts

Juice all the ingredients and serve in a tall glass. Decorate with a sprinkle of alfalfa sprouts, if liked.

Makes 250 ml (8 fl oz)

red eye

2 large tomatoes, about 200 g (7 oz)
1 small fennel bulb
10 g (½ oz) spring onion
10 g (½ oz) coriander
black pepper
Tabasco sauce

Juice the tomatoes, fennel, spring onion and coriander together before serving with black pepper and a splash of Tabasco sauce.

Makes 200 ml (7 fl oz)

papaya flyer

mellow yellow

kiwi quencher

purple passion

250 g (8 oz) blueberries
½ grapefruit
2 large apples
2.5 cm (1 inch) cube fresh root ginger, roughly chopped

Juice all the ingredients together and serve in a tall glass with ice cubes. Decorate with thin slices of ginger, if liked.

Makes 200 ml (7 fl oz)

easy does it

2 small pears
125 g (4 oz) watercress
½ lemon

Juice all the ingredients and serve in a small glass over ice. Add a twist of lemon, if liked.

Makes 50 ml (2 fl oz)

peach fizz

2 peaches
2.5 cm (1 inch) cube fresh root ginger, roughly chopped
sparkling mineral water

Juice the peach and ginger and serve in a tall glass over ice. Add a splash of sparkling water, a couple of mint leaves and slices of peach, if liked.

Makes 200 ml (7 fl oz)

strawberry sunrise

200 g (7 oz) strawberries
2 small oranges

Juice the strawberries and oranges. Serve straight over ice, or blend with a couple of ice cubes for a thicker drink. Decorate with whole strawberries, if liked.

Makes 200 ml (7 fl oz)

way to go

2 small pears
25 g (1 oz) pitted prunes
125 g (4 oz) spinach

Juice all the ingredients and serve in a glass over ice cubes. Decorate with pear slices, if liked.

Makes 200 ml (7 fl oz)

hazy days

1 large pear
100 ml (3½ fl oz) cranberry juice

Juice the pear and mix with the cranberry juice. Serve in a tall glass over ice and decorate with cranberries, if liked.

Makes 200 ml (7 fl oz)

hazy days

way to go

peach fizz

purple passion

morning after

¼ papaya
2 oranges
125 g (4 oz) cucumber

Juice the papaya flesh and orange (with as much pith as possible) with the cucumber and serve in a tall glass over ice. Decorate with slices of cucumber and papaya, if liked.

Makes 200 ml (7 fl oz)

quantum leap

2 large apples
2.5 cm (1 inch) cube fresh root ginger, roughly chopped

Juice the apple and ginger and serve in a glass over ice. Decorate with some chopped mint, if liked. This drink can be diluted with sparkling mineral water to taste.

Makes 100 ml (3½ fl oz)

c breeze

½ grapefruit
½ kiwifruit
¼ pineapple, about 175 g (6 oz)
50 g (2 oz) frozen raspberries
50 g (2 oz) frozen cranberries

Juice the grapefruit, kiwifruit and pineapple then whizz in a blender with the frozen berries to make a thick smoothie. Decorate with raspberries, if liked, and serve with straws.

Makes 200 ml (7 fl oz)

ginger spice

3 carrots
½ small fennel bulb
1 large celery stick
2.5 cm (1 inch) cube fresh root ginger, roughly chopped
1 tablespoon spirulina (optional)

Juice the ingredients and serve over ice. If liked, decorate with strips of fennel and fennel fronds. Add 1 tablespoon of spirulina if you want to suppress your appetite.

Makes 200 ml (7 fl oz)

morning after

ginger spice

green peace

100 g (3½ oz) broccoli
100 g (3½ oz) kale
25 g (1 oz) parsley
2 apples
1 celery stick

Juice all the ingredients and serve in a glass over ice. Decorate with sprigs of curly kale, if liked.

Makes 200 ml (7 fl oz)

full tank

¼ pineapple, about 100 g (3½ oz)
1 small apple
100 g (3½ oz) alfalfa sprouts
100 ml (3½ fl oz) soya milk

Juice the pineapple, apple and alfalfa sprouts together. Put the juice into a blender with the soya milk and an ice cube and blend. Serve in a tall glass.

Makes 300 ml (½ pint)

morning glory

½ cantaloupe melon (or any melon)

Juice the melon flesh and seeds for an enlivening breakfast drink then serve over ice. Drink immediately.

Makes 300 ml (½ pint)

apple and blackberry

3 apples
150 g (5 oz) blackberries
300 ml (½ pint) water

Juice the fruit then stir in the water. Pour into a glass and add a couple of ice cubes to chill.

Makes 600 ml (1 pint)

full tank

morning glory

eye opener

2 carrots
1 fennel bulb

Juice the carrots and fennel. Serve the juice in a tall glass over ice and garnished with fennel, if liked.

Makes 200 ml (7 fl oz)

pink grapefruit and pineapple

1 pink grapefruit
½ pineapple, about 225 g (7½ oz)
300 ml (½ pint) water

Juice the grapefruit and pineapple, then stir in the water. Pour into 2 glasses and add a couple of ice cubes to each glass.

Makes 600 ml (1 pint)

strawberry and kiwifruit

150 g (5 oz) strawberries, hulled
2 kiwifruit, peeled

Juice the strawberries and kiwifruit flesh together. Pour into a glass and add ice cubes, if liked.

Makes 300 ml (½ pint)

water baby

¼ watermelon, about 300 g (10 oz) flesh
125 g (4 oz) raspberries

Juice the watermelon flesh and raspberries, pour into a large glass and add a couple of ice cubes.

Makes 350 ml (12 fl oz)

water baby

eye opener

tummy tickler

3 small apples
200 g (7 oz) blackcurrants

Juice the fruit and serve over ice for a great blackcurrant cordial substitute. Decorate with extra blackcurrants, if liked.

Makes 200 ml (7 fl oz)

morning dew

3 celery sticks
¼ Galia or honeydew melon

Juice both ingredients to make a sweetly refreshing drink and serve with a twist of lemon.

Makes 200 ml (7 fl oz)

berry nice

2 bananas
200 g (7 oz) raspberries
125 g (4 oz) blueberries
1 small glass cranberry juice
2 tablespoons natural yogurt (optional)

Roughly chop the bananas and put into a blender. Add the berries and pour in the cranberry juice. Blend until smooth. Add the yogurt for a thicker creamier drink.

Makes 300 ml (½ pint)

bumpy ride

2 small apples
1 small beetroot, about 50 g (2 oz)
2 celery sticks

Juice all the ingredients and serve over ice in a tumbler. Decorate with apple slices, if liked.

Makes 150 ml (¼ pint)

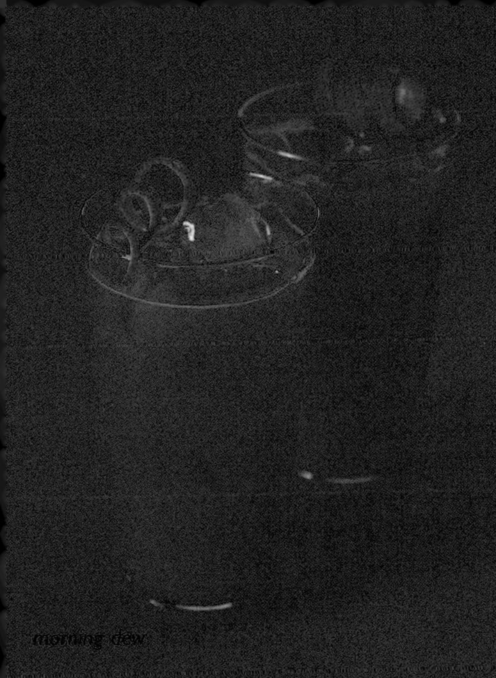

morning dew

bumpy ride

Here's to Good Health

clear ahead (see page [illegible])

grapple juice

1 apple
100 g (3½ oz) green grapes

Juice both ingredients for a simple, healthy drink then serve over ice. Decorate with apple slices, if liked.

Makes 200 ml (7 fl oz)

carrot and kiwifruit

2 carrots
1 kiwifruit

Juice the carrots and kiwifruit. Pour into a glass and add a couple of ice cubes. Decorate with slices of kiwifruit, if liked.

Makes 250 ml (8 fl oz)

red devil

½ large tomato, about 100 g (3½ oz)
¼ Galia or honeydew melon
1 carrot

Juice the tomato, melon flesh and carrot and serve over ice with fresh chillies, if liked.

Makes 250 ml (8 fl oz)

purple heart

2 small beetroot, about 100g (3½ oz)
¼ melon (any type)
2 small plums

Juice all the ingredients and then transfer to a blender. Add an ice cube and whizz for a thicker drink. Serve in a tall glass.

Makes 300 ml (½ pint)

purple heart

red devil

beetnik

2 small beetroot, about 100g (3½ oz)
50 g (2 oz) grapes
1 orange

Juice all ingredients and serve in a tumbler with ice to chill. Decorate with an orange slice, if liked.

Makes 200 ml (7 fl oz)

city slicker

1 parsnip
1 fennel bulb
200 g (7 oz) cucumber

Juice all the ingredients and serve over ice with mint, if liked.

Makes 200 ml (7 fl oz)

grape expectation

½ small pear
50 g (2 oz) red grapes
50 g (2 oz) blackberries

Juice the fruit together and serve over ice.

Makes 200 ml (7 fl oz)

mr green

200 g (7 oz) broccoli
200 g (7 oz) green grapes

Juice both ingredients and serve over ice, garnished with mint.

Makes 200 ml (7 fl oz)

mystic mango

100 g (3½ oz) green grapes
1 small fennel bulb
½ large mango

Juice the grapes and fennel then put into a blender with the mango and a couple of ice cubes and blend to make a replenishing icy smoothie. Serve with fennel fronds, if liked.

Makes 300 ml (½ pint)

beetnik

mystic mango

city slicker

fireball

100 g (3½ oz) raspberries
1 small fennel bulb
1 small pear
2.5 cm (1 inch) cube fresh root ginger, roughly chopped

Juice all the ingredients together to make a sweet, spicy drink and serve.

Makes 200 ml (7 fl oz)

autumn leaf

1 small peach
2 celery sticks
1 small orange

Juice the peach, celery and orange together and serve poured over ice. Decorate with slices of peach, if liked.

Makes 200 ml (7 fl oz)

orangatang

1 small orange
1 carrot
½ sweet potato
2.5 cm (1 inch) cube fresh root ginger, roughly chopped

Juice the orange with the carrot, sweet potato and ginger. Serve poured over ice. Decorate with a slice of orange, if liked.

Makes 200 ml (7 fl oz)

slow burn

1 celery stick
¼ parsnip
50 g (2 oz) pineapple
50 g (2 oz) lettuce
50 g (2 oz) grapes

Juice all the ingredients together and serve in a short tumbler. Serve with slivers of pineapple, if liked.

Makes 150 ml (¼ pint)

autumn leaf

orangatang

slow burn

panic attack

2 apples
3 apricots
1 peach

Juice the apples, apricots and peach. Pour into a blender with a few ice cubes and whizz for 10 seconds. Serve in a tall glass and decorate with peach slices, if liked.

Makes 200 ml (7 fl oz)

culture shock

2 large apples
100 g (3½ oz) frozen cranberries
100 g (3½ oz) live natural yogurt
1 tablespoon clear honey

Juice the apple and whizz in a blender with the other ingredients for a fresh-tasting smoothie. Serve in a tumbler over ice cubes.

Makes 200 ml (7 fl oz)

passion thriller

½ Galia or honeydew melon
125 g (4 oz) cucumber
1 small avocado
50 g (2 oz) dried apricots
1 tablespoon wheatgerm

Juice the melon and cucumber. Whizz in a blender with the avocado, apricots, wheatgerm and a couple of ice cubes. Decorate with dried apricot slivers, if liked.

Makes 200 ml (7 fl oz)

clear ahead

2 large carrots
50 g (2 oz) radishes
1 large apple

Juice the carrots, radishes and apple. Pour the juice into a blender and process with a couple of ice cubes. Serve decorated with slices of apple, if liked.

Makes 200 ml (7 fl oz)

panic attack

passion thriller

culture shock

clear ahead

summer breeze

⅓ Galia melon
1 small fennel bulb

Juice both ingredients for a light fresh drink and serve over ice. Serve with slivers of fennel, if liked.

Makes 200 ml (7 fl oz)

pick-me-up

2 carrots
1 tart-flavoured apple, such as Granny Smith
1 cm (½ inch) piece fresh root ginger, roughly chopped

Juice the carrots, apple and ginger. Pour into a glass and add a couple of ice cubes, and decorate with apple, if liked.

Makes 250 ml (8 fl oz)

carrot, orange and apple

2 carrots
1 orange
1 tart-flavoured apple, such as Granny Smith

Juice all the fruit, pour into a glass then add a couple of ice cubes.

Makes 250 ml (8 fl oz)

summer breeze

pick-me-up

celery and tomato

2 celery sticks
4 tomatoes
large handful of parsley
½ lemon, rind and juice

Feed the celery, tomato and parsley into the juicer in alternate batches, along with the lemon juice and rind. Pour the juice into a glass and add a couple of ice cubes.

Makes 300 ml (½ pint)

ultimate detox

4 carrots
2 green apples

Juice both the ingredients and serve in a tall glass over ice for a great clensing drink. Decorate with slices of apple, if liked.

Makes 300 ml (½ pint)

strawberry, peach and apple

125 g (4 oz) strawberries, hulled
2 peaches
1 red apple
300 ml (½ pint) water

Juice the strawberries, peaches and apple. Add the water and mix well, then pour the juice into a glass and add ice cubes, if liked.

Makes 600 ml (1 pint)

scarlet woman

2 small beetroot, about 100 g (3½ oz)
100 g (3½ oz) strawberries
1 small apple

Juice all the ingredients and serve decorated with a twist of apple peel, if liked.

Makes 300 ml (½ pint)

ultimate detox

scarlet woman

flush-a-bye-baby

250 g (8 oz) cranberries
¼ watermelon or ½ Galia melon
250 g (8 oz) cucumber

Juice all the ingredients, including the pips of the melon and the skin of the cucumber. Serve in a tumbler and decorate with melon sticks, if liked.

Makes 200 ml (7 fl oz)

healing hand

2 pears
3 kiwifruit, peeled
½ lime

Use ripe pears, if possible. Juice them with the kiwifruit flesh. Pour into a glass, add a couple of ice cubes and decorate with slices of kiwifruit, if liked.

Makes 300 ml (½ pint)

red-hot remedy

4 large tomatoes
1 apple
1 celery stick
4 basil leaves, finely chopped
1½ tablespoons lime juice

Juice the tomatoes, apple and celery. Pour into a glass over ice, and stir in the basil and lime juice.

Makes 200 ml (7 fl oz)

apple and plum

5 dessert plums
3 red apples

Choose ripe plums if possible. Juice them with the apple and serve in a glass poured over a couple of ice cubes.

Makes 300 ml (½ pint)

healing hand

flush-a-bye-baby

Hi-Energy Boosters

juicy lucy (see page 120)

back on track

1 small sweet potato
2 small oranges
1 large carrot

Juice the sweet potato, oranges and carrots. To make a smoother, creamier drink, transfer the juice to a blender and process with a couple of ice cubes. Decorate with mint sprigs, if liked.

Makes 200 ml (7 fl oz)

evergreen

1 celery stick
50 g (2 oz) fennel
125 g (4 oz) Romaine lettuce
½ pineapple, about 225 g (7½ oz)
1 teaspoon chopped tarragon

Juice all the ingredients and whizz in a blender with 2 ice cubes. Serve in a tall glass, decorated with tarragon sprigs, if liked.

Makes 200 ml (7 fl oz)

power pack

3 small carrots
2 beetroot, about 125 g (4 oz)
1 orange
125 g (4 oz) strawberries

Juice the carrots, beetroots and orange together. Put the juice into a blender with a couple of ice cubes and the strawberries. Whizz for 20 seconds and serve in a tall glass. Decorate with strips of orange rind, if liked.

Makes 200 ml (7 fl oz)

grape and plum

150 g (5 oz) seedless red grapes
5 plums

Juice the grapes and plums together, and pour into a glass. Add a couple of ice cubes and decorate with slices of plum, if liked.

Makes 300 ml (½ pint)

back on track

evergreen

power pack

liven up

½ Galia melon
½ pineapple, about 225 g (7½ oz)
1 green apple

Juice the flesh of the melon and pineapple with the apple. Pour into a glass and add a couple of ice cubes. Decorate with apple slices, if liked.

Makes 300 ml (½ pint)

red velvet

½ large red pepper, deseeded
125 g (4 oz) strawberries
½ small tomato, about 50 g (2 oz)
½ large mango
⅛ watermelon, about 125 g (4 oz) flesh

Juice all the ingredients, then whizz in a blender with 3 ice cubes and serve in a tall glass. Decorate with mango slices, if liked.

Makes 200 ml (7 fl oz)

magnificent 7

1 carrot
½ green pepper, seeded
25 g (1 oz) spinach
25 g (1 oz) onion
1 celery stick
90 g (3 oz) cucumber
½ small tomato, about 50 g (2 oz)
sea salt and pepper

Juice the ingredients and season with sea salt and pepper for the ultimate healthy pick-me-up. If liked, decorate with tomato quarters.

Makes 200 ml (7 fl oz)

high kick

250 g (8 oz) strawberries
1 kiwifruit
½ large banana
1 tablespoon spirulina
1 tablespoon linseeds

Juice the strawberries and kiwifruit and whizz in a blender with the banana, spirulina, linseeds and a couple of ice cubes. Decorate with redcurrants and linseeds, if liked.

Makes 200 ml (7 fl oz)

liven up

red velvet

high kick

watercress and pear

3 pears
40 g (1½ oz) watercress

Choose ripe pears if possible. Feed the pear chunks and watercress into the juicer in alternate batches. Pour into a glass and add ice cubes. Decorate with watercress leaves, if liked.

Makes 250 ml (8 fl oz)

energy bubble

3 apples, preferably red
1 mango
2 passion fruit

Juice the apples and mango with the passion fruit flesh (discard the seeds). Pour the juice into a glass and add a couple of ice cubes. Decorate with apple slices, if liked.

Makes 300 ml (½ pint)

beetroot, apple and carrot

2 small beetroot, about 100 g (3½ oz)
1 carrot
2 apples
300 ml (½ pint) water

Juice the beetroot, carrot and apples. Add the water, mix well then pour into a glass. Add a couple of ice cubes to chill.

Makes 600 ml (1 pint)

celery, tomato and red pepper

3 tomatoes, about 500 g (1 lb)
4 celery sticks
½ red pepper, deseeded
½ red chilli, deseeded (optional)
1 garlic clove, crushed (optional)

Choose ripe tomatoes if possible. Juice them with the celery and red pepper. Pour into a glass, stir in the chilli and crushed garlic, if using, and add a couple of ice cubes, if liked.

Makes 300 ml (½ pint)

watercress and pear

energy bubble

celery, tomato and red pepper

sky high

½ lime, unpeeled
2 pears
½ pineapple, about 225 g (7½ oz)

Scrub the lime and juice it with the pears and pineapple flesh. Pour into a glass, add a couple of ice cubes and decorate with pinapple, if liked.

Makes 300 ml (½ pint)

energy burst

125 g (4 oz) spinach
2 large apples
½ yellow pepper, deseeded
a pinch of cinnamon

Juice all the ingredients for a fatigue-fighting drink and serve in a tall glass. If liked, add cinnamon sticks for decoration.

Makes 200 ml (7 fl oz)

red wire

100 g (3½ oz) red grapes
2 small beetroot, about 100 g (3½ oz)
2 small plums

Juice the grapes, beetroot and plums together and serve in a tumbler over ice. Decorate with plum slices, if liked.

Makes 200 ml (7 fl oz)

energy burst

red wire

sky high

melon, kiwifruit and grape

½ honeydew melon
2 kiwifruit, peeled
125 g (4 oz) seedless green grapes

Juice the flesh of the melon and kiwifruit with the grapes. Pour into a glass and add ice cubes. Serve with slices of kiwifruit, if liked.

Makes 300 ml (½ pint)

whizzical

1 banana
200 ml (7 fl oz) soya milk
50 g (2 oz) ground almonds

Put all the ingredients in a blender with 2 ice cubes and blend until smooth. Serve sprinkled with cinnamon flakes, if liked.

Makes 300 ml (½ pint)

marathon man

½ Galia melon
175 g (6 oz) seedless green grapes
300 ml (½ pint) water

Juice the melon flesh with the grapes. Mix in the water and pour into 2 glasses. Add a couple of ice cubes and decorate with grapes, if liked.

Makes 600 ml (1 pint)

marathon man

whizzical

melon, kiwifruit and grape

deep breath

1 large tomato, about 200 g (7 oz)
½ red pepper, deseeded
¼ papaya

Juice the tomato, red pepper and papaya flesh. Pour the juice into a food processor or blender, add a couple of ice cubes and process. Serve decorated with slivers of red pepper, if liked.

Makes 200 ml (7 fl oz)

raw energy

1 small tomato, about 100 g (3½ oz)
200 g (7 oz) cabbage
large handful of parsley
1 celery stick (optional)

Juice the tomato, cabbage and parsley together and serve in a tumbler. Add sliced tomatoes or a stick of celery, to garnish.

Makes 200 ml (7 fl oz)

invigorate

2 oranges
½ lemon
1 cm (½ inch) cube fresh root ginger, roughly chopped
2 small beetroot, about 100 g (3½ oz)
100 g (3½ oz) spinach
2 celery sticks
1 carrot

Juice all the ingredients together. Serve decorated with orange rind curls, if liked.

Makes 600 ml (1 pint)

red rocket

2 small carrots
2 large apples
125 g (4 oz) red cabbage

Juice all the ingredients together. Serve over ice in a tall glass and decorate with slivers of red cabbage, if liked.

Makes 200 ml (7 fl oz)

deep breath

invigorate

red rocket

raw energy

battery charge

2 kiwifruit, peeled
300 g (10 oz) seedless green grapes

Juice the kiwifruit flesh with the grapes. Pour the juice into a glass and add some crushed ice. Decorate with kiwifruit, if liked.

Makes 300 ml (½ pint)

juicy lucy

½ watermelon, about 225 g (7½ oz) flesh
200 g (7 oz) strawberries

Juice the fruit and whizz in a blender with a couple of ice cubes. Serve decorated with mint leaves and whole or sliced strawberries, if liked.

Makes 200 ml (7 fl oz)

celery, apple and alfalfa

3 celery sticks
2 tart-flavoured apples, such as Granny Smith
25 g (1 oz) alfalfa sprouts

Feed all the ingredients into a juicer in alternate batches. Pour into a glass, add a couple of ice cubes and drink immediately.

Makes 250 ml (8 fl oz)

kale and hearty

25 g (1 oz) kale
100 g (3½ oz) wheatgrass
1 teaspoon spirulina

Juice the kale and the wheatgrass then stir in the spirulina powder. Serve in a small glass decorated with wheatgrass blades.

Makes 50 ml (2 fl oz)

battery charge

kale and hearty

juicy lucy

Index of Juices and Smoothies

Index of Ingredients

Acknowledgements

The publisher would like to thank UK Juicers, 29b Mill Lane, Acaster Malbis, York, YO23 2UJ (tel: 01904 704705) www.ukjuicers.com for the loan of the Greenstar Juicer.

Executive Editor: Nicola Hill
Editor: Jessica Cowie
Executive Art Editor: Geoff Fennell
Designer: Sue Michniewiz
Production Controller: Viv Cracknell
Photographer: Stephen Conroy
Home Economist: David Morgan
Stylist: Angela Swaffield

Juice recipes written by
Amanda Cross and **Fiona Hunter**